ALNWICK

CW00433680

After Newcastle, Alnwick used to be the second an̄o
size and importance. But it remained unaffected by
which transformed the towns of Tyneside. Today it stul remains much as it must
have appeared to the stage coach passengers travelling between Newcastle and
Edinburgh.

It was probably occupied by prehistoric peoples since camps, dwellings and
burial grounds abound in the neighbourhood. The River Aln itself is a Celtic
name. It was a centre of communications in prehistoric times and probably for
this reason became an important Anglican centre, 'the wic (farmstead) on the
Aln'. Little, however, is known of the town before the Norman Conquest. The
building of a castle in the 12th century set the pattern of Alnwick's
development. The construction of a baronial stronghold controlling a vital river
crossing was the dominant influence on the growth of the town.

Alnwick Castle, 1832

THE CASTLE

The first castle at Alnwick was a motte-and-bailey and enclosed an area of about seven acres. There may have been a Saxon castle on the site but no evidence of it exists. It is probable that the first Norman owner was Gilbert Tyson, William the Conqueror's standard bearer at the battle of Hastings. It seems that Tyson was deprived of his lands owing to his participation in Mowbray's rebellion against William in 1095. In any case Yvo de Vescy became owner after 1096 and he seems to have erected the earliest parts of the present castle. A shell keep was built on the levelled motte in the early 12th century with two baileys one on the east and one on the west. There are remains of the motte and its retaining wall around the keep.

In 1138, Alnwick, then belonging to Eustace Fitz John, is described as a most powerful castle – *munitissimum castellum* – and much of the masonry of the curtain wall agrees with this date. Eustace Fitz John had taken over Alnwick by marriage to Beatrix, the only daughter of Yvo de Vescy. He was a large landowner who played an important part in public affairs. He continued with the fortification of the castle and the Norman arch leading to the inner ward was his work. The castle at this time was substantially the same design as at present. He was succeeded by his son William who successfully defended the castle in 1172 against William the Lion, King of Scotland. Two years later the castle was once again besieged by the Scottish king who was surprised by a relieving force and taken prisoner. A stone near the main entrance to Alnwick Park marks the spot where the king was captured.

In the year 1309 a new era in the history of the castle starts with its purchase by Sir Henry de Percy. At the time the estates of the de Vescys were held in trust for a minor of the family by Anthony Bek, Bishop of Durham. It is said he unscrupulously sold the estates to the Percy family. The Percy family was descended from William de Percy who had accompanied William the Conqueror in 1066 and had been granted estates in Yorkshire, Lincolnshire and Sussex. They were one of the most powerful families in England.

The first Lord Percy of Alnwick began to restore and strengthen the castle without altering its general form and design, then reconstructed the keep with seven semicircular towers round an irregular court. He repaired the curtain wall adding strong towers such as the Constables, the Postern in the middle bailey, the Abbots, the Western and Eastern Garrets, the Auditor's and part of the Record Tower. He also built the great barbican of the outer bailey and it is his motto – *Esperaunce* – which appears on its front. The mason's marks on some of these buildings are the same as those at Dunstanburgh so it seems that the same workmen were employed at both castles. His son (1315-1352) continued the work of restoration. He added the two lofty towers guarding the entrance to the inner bailey. The money to build these towers is said to have come from the ransoms of the Scottish prisoners taken at the battle of Neville's Cross. The shield containing the Royal Arms above the keep entrance is reported to commemorate Edward III's visit in 1335.

Barbican, Alnwick Castle   T. M. Richardson

At this time the regular garrison of the castle was three knights, thirty-seven esquires, and forty hobelars or light cavalry, along with men-at-arms. The constable in command received £326 9s. 10d. per annum. The wages of the garrison were £1,137 yearly, the men-at-arms receiving 12d. a day and the hobelars 6d. The cost of victualling, repairs and munitions was £1,256.

At the Coronation of Richard II the 4th Lord Percy was made Earl of Northumberland. His son Hotspur was a well-known figure in Border warfare. He was the leader of the English at the Battle of Otterburn, took part in the battle of Homildon Hill, and was killed at Shrewsbury while in revolt against the King. As a traitor his body was drawn and quartered. After the death of his father at Bramham Moor the estates were forfeited for a time but eleven earls followed before the male Percy line became extinct. The 5th Earl of Northumberland (1489-1527) was known as 'The Magnificent' on account of the splendour of his establishment and his love of display. At his marriage we are told his splendour exceeded all the nobility present. He outdid them "for the richness of his coat, being goldsmith's work garnished with pearle and stones; and for the costly apparel of his henxmen, and gallant trappers of their horses, besides four hundred tall men well horsed, and apparalled in his colours. He was esteemed both of the Scots and Englishmen more like a prince than a subject".

Probably the most interesting thing for us that has survived from the time of the 5th Earl is his Household Book which gives us a picture of life in a large baronial castle in the early 16th century. Here are some of the curious particulars extracted by William Davison.

"The family consists of 166 persons, masters and servants; fifty-seven strangers are reckoned upon every day. Twopence halfpenny is supposed to be the daily expense of each for meat, drink and firing.

"The whole expense of the Earl's family is managed with an exactness that is very rigid, such as may seem to border on an extreme; insomuch, that the number of pieces which must be cut out of every quarter of beef, mutton, pork, veal, nay stock-fish and salmon, are determined, and must be entered and accounted for by the different clerks appointed for that purpose.

"If a servant be absent a day, his mess is struck off. If he go on my Lord's business, board-wages are allowed him; eightpence a day for his journey in winter, and fivepence in summer.

"One hundred and nine fat beeves are bought at All-hallow tide, at thirteen shillings and fourpence a piece; and twenty-four lean beeves to be bought at St Helens, at eight shillings a piece. These are to be put into the pastures to feed, and are to serve from Midsummer to Michaelmas, which is consequently the only time that the family eats fresh beef. During the rest of the year they live on salted meat.

"One hundred and sixty gallons of mustard are allowed in the year; which seems indeed requisite for the salt beef. Six hundred and forty-seven sheep are allowed, at twenty-pence each.

"Only twenty-five hogs are allowed, at two shillings each; twenty-eight veals at twenty-pence; forty lambs at a shilling. These seem to be reserved for my Lord's table or that of the upper servants, called the knights' table; the other servants, as they eat salted meat almost through the whole year, and with few or no vegetables, had a very bad and unhealthy diet.

"We must entertain as mean an idea of their cleanliness. Only seventy ells of linen, at eightpence an ell, are annually allowed for this great family. No sheets are allowed. This linen was made into eight table-cloths for my Lord's table and a table-cloth for the knights. This last was probably only washed once a month. Only forty shillings are allowed for washing throughout the whole year; and most of it seems expended on the linen belonging to the chapel.

"The drinking, however, was tolerable, namely, ten tuns and two hogs heads of Gascony wine, at the rate of £41 13s. 4d. a tun; only ninety-one dozen of candles for the whole year.

"The family rose at six in the morning, dined at ten, and supped at four in the afternoon. The gates were all shut at nine, and no further ingress nor egress was allowed.

"My Lord and Lady have set on their table for breakfast, at seven o'clock in the morning, a quart of beer, as much wine, two pieces of salt fish, six red-herrings, four white ones, and a dish of sprats. On flesh-days half a chyne of mutton, or a chyne of boiled beef.

"Mass is ordered to be said at six o'clock, in order, says the household book, that all my Lord's servants may rise early.

"My Lord keeps only twenty-seven horses at his own charge; his upper servants have allowance for maintaining their own horses. These horses are, six gentle horses, as they are called, at hay and hard meat throughout the year; four palfries, three hobbies and nags, three sumpter horses; six horses for those servants for whom my Lord furnishes a horse, two sumpter horses more, and three mill-horses, two for carrying the corn, and one for grinding it. Besides these, there are seven great trotting horses for the chariot or waggon. He allows a peck of oats a day, besides loaves made of beans, for his principal horses; the oats at twenty-pence, the beans at two shillings a quarter. The load of hay is at two shillings and eightpence. When my Lord is on a journey, he carries thirty-six horses along with him, together with bed and other accommodation. The inns, it seems, could afford nothing tolerable.

"My Lord passes the year in three country seats, all in Yorkshire; but he has furniture only for one; he carries everything along with him, beds, tables, chairs, kitchen utensils, all of which we may conclude were so coarse that they could not be spoiled by the carriage; yet seventeen carts and one waggon suffice for the whole.

"One remarkable circumstance is that he has seven priests in his house, besides seventeen persons, chanters, musicians, etc., belonging to his chapel; yet

THE SOUTH EAST VIEW OF ALNWICK CASTLE IN NORTHUMBERLAND.

To the Right Hon.ble ALGERNON Earl of Northumberland, Baron Percy &c. Wars Aylworth who is now the Duke of Somerset, Lord Lieutenant and Custos Rotulorum of the County of Sussex Captain of the Horse Troop of his Guards, and Governour of Tynemouth Castle.

This Prospect is humbly Inscribed by ___

Your Lordships most Obedient humble Serv.ts

Sam.l & Nath.l Buck.

he has only two cooks for a family of two hundred and twenty-three persons.

"Their meals were certainly dressed in the slovenly manner of a ship's company. It is amusing to observe the pompous and even royal style assumed by this Tartar Chief. he does not give any order, though only for the right making of mustard, but it is used with this preamble: 'It seemeth good to us and our council'.

"Yet the Earl is sometimes not deficient in generosity: he pays, for instance, an annual pension of a groat (4d.) a year, to my lady of Walsingham, for her interest in heaven, and the same sum to the holy blood at Hales.

"No mention is anywhere made of plate, but only of the hiring of pewter vessels. The servants seem all to have bought their own clothes from their wages. Neither is any glass mentioned. It only came in use about 1557."

We need only mention here a few of the earls. Henry the 9th Earl (1585-1632) known as the 'Wizard Earl', on account of his interest in chemistry and astronomy, made Alnwick his principal seat. He was the only one of the earls to do so, since the others had always preferred Warkworth as a residence. Although Alnwick was the chief military stronghold his son Algernon decided not to live in Northumberland and from this time until the 18th century the Percys ceased to play an important part in the North but continued living in the South. By 1635 the castle had fallen into a sad state of repair which the Civil War accelerated. In 1650 after the battle of Dunbar 6,000 prisoners were confined in the castle and half died from starvation within eight days. Another 2,000 perished on their journey from Alnwick to Durham.

A statue on the castle walls

Hotspur's Seat, Record Tower

West Garret, Abbot's Tower, Falconer's Tower

Avener's Tower, Barbican from the interior

Constable's Tower

Alnwick Castle in the 18th century

In 1722 Algernon, Duke of Somerset, succeeded to the Barony of Percy, and frequently stayed at Alnwick. His only daughter Elizabeth married Sir Hugh Smithson, a Yorkshire baronet, who became the owner of the estates in Northumberland and also succeeded in 1750 to the title of Earl of Northumberland (he was created Duke of Northumberland in 1766). He was a capable business man and introduced modern methods on all his estates. He decided to restore Alnwick castle. Work probably started in 1755 and was completed in 1766. The architect was the famous Robert Adam who changed the baronial fortress into a splendid mansion in the pseudo-Gothic style. Some of the work, like the fine fan-shaped staircase, was attractive but the overall effect was atrocious. The blame for the mess created is usually placed on the Duchess since the Duke was said to be a man of taste.

Fortunately Algernon the fourth Duke (1847-1865) decided to sweep away the work of Adam. In 1854 he started with Salvin as architect, to restore the castle outwardly to its medieval state but internally to have a comfortable residence. Salvin wanted to have the interior done in the medieval style but the Duke decided to adopt Italian renaissance decoration. For this he employed famous Italian architects and artists. More than 300 workmen were employed on the work. To give the English workmen the necessary skill schools of drawing, carving and plaster decorating were started in the castle. The result is the magnificent interior we see today since only minor alterations have taken place since the 19th century restoration was completed.

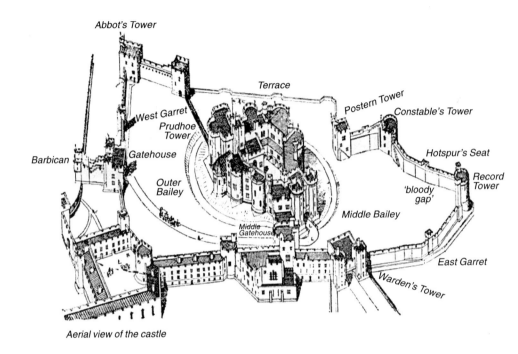

Aerial view of the castle

Labels on image: Abbot's Tower, Terrace, Postern Tower, Constable's Tower, West Garret, Prudhoe Tower, Hotspur's Seat, Barbican, Gatehouse, Record Tower, Outer Bailey, 'bloody gap', Middle Bailey, Middle Gatehouse, East Garret, Warden's Tower

Description of the castle

The visitor enters the castle from Narrowgate. The main entrance is a strong gatehouse with the barbican in front built about 1440. Between the barbican and gatehouse is a moat, formerly supplied with water from the Bow Burn, but now dry.

On passing through the gatehouse we enter the outer bailey. In front is the keep with a chapel with a pointed roof and the Prudhoe Tower. Both were built in 1854. The rest of the keep seen here was restored about 1764. The curtain wall on the left runs north to the Abbot's Tower with a small watch tower between called the Western Garret. This section of wall is mainly early 14th century work. The wall from the Abbot's to the Falconer's Tower is early 12th century masonry but the tower itself is 19th century restoration. The wall to the south from the gatehouse leads to the Avener's and Black Towers. Most of this section is 18th century work as well as the stable yard which was built on the site of the old moat. The wall on the south which includes the Auditor's Tower is completely medieval. We are told this tower received its name because the 6th Earl imprisoned one of his auditors here, a man called William Worme, "until he has accounted for more money received than ever I received".

Passing through the middle gateway the visitor enters the middle bailey. Here the curtain wall leading to the Warden's Tower is 19th century as is the tower itself but the next long stretch to the Record Tower is early work with a 14th century tower in the middle called the Eastern Garret. From the Record

The well, Alnwick Castle

Norman gateway, Alnwick Castle

Tower (built 1885) to the Constable's Tower (built c.1310) is a mainly modern section of wall with a small 14th century turret known as Hotspur's Seat. Part of the wall is referred to as the 'bloody gap' from an apocryphal breach made here by the Scots. The Constable's Tower was built c.1310 and has never been altered. It was the residence of the constable of the castle. From here the 14th century wall runs to the Postern Tower. Underneath this is the postern door or sally-port, the only other entrance to the castle in the Middle Ages. This tower, now used as a museum, was built c.1310 and is practically untouched. Beyond this tower lies a terrace made in the 18th and 19th centuries on which are placed several guns.

The keep was surrounded by a dry moat. The entrance is between the two great octagonal towers which are the finest feature of the castle. They were built c.1350 by Henry, the 2nd Earl Percy, and the thirteen armorial shields displayed are families connected with him. The stone figures on the battlements are original. Apart from the middle gateway all the other stone figures on the castle battlements were added in the 18th century. On entering the inner bailey we see mainly 18th century work although the well is original 14th century. However, the statue of the saint blessing the water is an 18th century ornamentation. The interior of the keep is the work of the 4th Duke (1854-1865) and, although magnificent Italian work, need not detain us here since it is fully described in the official guide book.

Inner Bailey, Alnwick Castle

Tysen De Vesci Clifford

Arundel Bohun Lancaster

Warren Percy Umfreville

Percy Neville Fitzwalter

Coats of arms of the owners of Alnwick Castle

14

ALNWICK TOWN WALLS

Prior to the middle of the 15th century, Alnwick was unwalled and on a number of occasions was sacked by the Scots. In 1433 a licence to enclose the town was granted by Henry VI. "It has been commonly represented that, soon afterwards, the Earl of Northumberland erected the walls of the town; this, however, is a

From Andrew Armstrong's map of Northumberland, 1769

*This map shows the towers at **B**ondgate, **C**layport and **P**ottergate*

myth, for little indeed he seems to have contributed to a work so important to the safety of the inhabitants, when border warfare was raging. The burden fell mainly on the burgesses and commonalty, who were poor enough in these evil times, hence for want of means the fortifying of the town made slow progress, and half a century elapsed before it was completed" (George Tate). Many documents exist showing how difficult it was to raise the necessary money. Grants were made from the Royal Exchequer and even from the Bishop of Norwich (who had been born in Alnwick) but no assistance was given by the Earls of Northumberland whose castle overlooked the town. When the walls were completed the entrances were defended by four strong towers. At the south was Bondgate, at the south-west Clayport, at the west Pottergate, and at the north Narrowgate. Only one tower remains today, that of Bondgate, which is often wrongly called 'Hotspur's Tower'. Hotspur was long dead before the tower was even started and his contribution to its building was nil.

Bondgate Tower has three storeys with an arched gateway. In a panel on the outside was a sculptured Brabant Lion, now scarcely visible. Semi-octagonal towers project on each side of the gateway while above are three corbels to support projecting wooden fortifications. The outside windows of the gate are long narrow slits but inside they are larger and mullioned. In 1557 it is described as "of thre houshe height besyd the batilment and faire turrett, yt ys covered with leade which ys in great decaye as also the roof of woode". In the 17th and 18th centuries it was occasionally used as a prison. Clayport Tower

Bondgate, also known as 'Hotspur's Tower'

was similar to Bondgate but larger. It became the meeting place of the incorporated trades and later the poor house. It was demolished in 1804 and the materials used for the erection of the Union Court in Clayport Street. Narrowgate Tower was at the end of the street at the commencement of Bailiffgate.

Pottergate Tower was demolished and a new tower erected in 1768. It was in the pseudo-Gothic style with a lanthorn resembling that of St Nicholas at Newcastle, built at a total cost of £580. The clock, taken from the Town Hall, was added a few years later. In 1812 the lanthorn was damaged in a storm and in spite of public protest was demolished instead of being repaired. Our illustration shows the tower as it was in 1812.

The town walls were 6.24m (20½ feet) high and 1.83m (6 feet) thick and ran for about one mile. The map of Alnwick by A. Armstrong, published in 1769, shows three of the towers: Bondgate, Clayport and Pottergate.

Pottergate Tower, 1812

HULNE PARK

ALNWICK ABBEY

In the magnificent Hulne Park the remains of Alnwick Abbey are well worth a visit. Crossing the bridge at the foot of Canongate the park is entered at the Abbey Lodge. A short distance from it are the remains of Alnwick Abbey, which was founded in 1147 by Eustace Fitz-John and his wife Beatrice for a colony of Premonstratensian or White Canons. It is believed to be the second abbey of this order to be founded in England. When it was founded it stood outside the Park and remained so for over six hundred years.

The history of the abbey is uneventful. It was wealthy and protected by the great castle nearby. One of the priors, in 1304, wrote a curious Latin poem on Robin Hood. This is the earliest record of the name of the popular hero. The monks also compiled a Chronicle which, like most monkish chronicles, is full of falsehoods and superstitious stories but contains some interesting historical information. The original manuscript has disappeared but a copy is preserved in the British Museum. The monks may not have been great writers, but they knew how to entertain. In the year 1376 they gave a magnificent banquet at which more than 1,000 guests were entertained. In the same year there was a great scarcity of corn and almost all the oxen and sheep belonging to the abbey perished in a pestilence.

The report on the abbey made in the reign of Henry VIII states, under the heading of superstition, that the canons held in veneration a foot of Simon de Montfort, and a cup of Saint Thomas of Canterbury. The foot was the most valued relic and was preserved in a shrine of purest silver shaped like a shoe. Many miracles are recorded concerning this foot.

When the house was dissolved in 1539 the number of canons was thirteen. The abbey soon became a ruin and a quarry for builders.

The Gatehouse of the Abbey

Of the original abbey not one stone is recognizable save the fortified entrance tower which was built in the 14th century. It is large with four strong projecting towers at the corners. A gateway with a round arch passes through. On the north front above the spring of the arch on each side is a square recess, now empty. Above the arch is a figure, probably an angel. Above are machicolations supported by corbels. On the merlons of the battlement are two shields of De Vescy. The south front is not machicolated and has the same De Vescy shields. In a niche above a mullioned window is a figure of a Premonstratensian canon.

Gateway of Alnwick Abbey, 1868

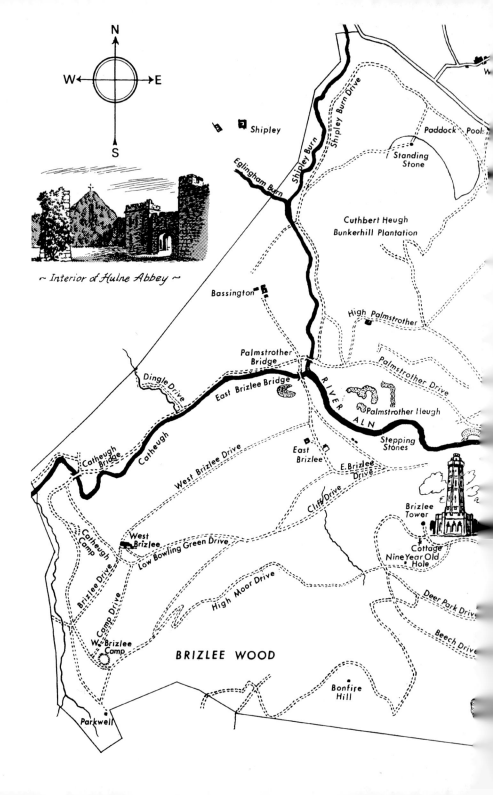

~ Interior of Hulne Abbey ~

N
W E
S

Shipley

Paddock · Pool

Shipley Burn

Shipley Burn Drive

Eglingham Burn

Standing Stone

Cuthbert Heugh
Bunkerhill Plantation

Bassington

High Palmstrother

Palmstrother Bridge

Palmstrother Drive

Dingle Drive

East Brizlee Bridge

RIVER

Palmstrother Heugh

ALN

Catheugh Bridge

Catheugh

West Brizlee Drive

East Brizlee

E. Brizlee Drive

Stepping Stones

Brizlee Tower

Catheugh Camp

West Brizlee

Low Bowling Green Drive

Cliff Drive

Cottage
Nine Year Old Hole

Brizlee Drive

Camp Drive

High Moor Drive

Deer Park Drive

Beech Drive

W. Brizlee Camp

BRIZLEE WOOD

Bonfire Hill

Parkwell

HULNE PARK
ALNWICK

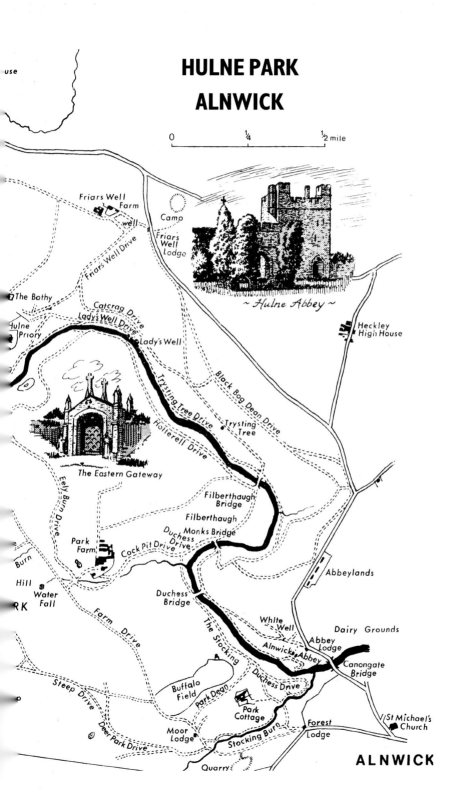

0   ¼   ½ mile

~ Hulne Abbey ~

...use

Friars Well Farm

well

Camp

Friars Well Lodge

Friars Well Drive

Heckley High House

The Bothy

Catcrag Drive

Lady's Well Drive

Hulne Priory

Lady's Well

Black Bog Dean Drive

Trysting Tree Drive

Trysting Tree

Hollerell Drive

The Eastern Gateway

Eely Burn Drive

Filberthaugh Bridge

Filberthaugh

Monks Bridge

Duchess Drive

Park Farm

Cock Pit Drive

Abbeylands

...Burn

Hill

Water Fall

Duchess Bridge

R K

Farm Drive

White Well

Dairy Grounds

The Stocking

Abbey Lodge

Alnwick Abbey

Canongate Bridge

Steep Drive

Buffalo Field

Park Dean

Duchess Drive

Park Cottage

St Michael's Church

Moor Lodge

Deer Park Drive

Stocking Burn

Forest Lodge

Quarry

ALNWICK

The eastern front is very ornamented. Above a blocked up entrance is a low arch resting on angels with extended wings. Above the arch is a shield with the Brabant Lion and three lucies quartered, arms adopted by the Percys about 1385. The same arms are on the projecting towers and the centre merlon of the battlement. The upper floor of the tower contains several long straight-headed two-light windows with transoms and big hood-moulds.

The foundations of the buildings of the abbey have been laid bare and the bases covered with cement so the ground plans of the various parts of the building can be seen.

The White Well, belonging to the canons, also remains. It is on the bank side a little to the north-west, and is covered by a small stone building.

HULNE PRIORY

Leaving Alnwick Abbey we follow the river for half-a-mile and cross it at the Monk's Bridge and a few hundred yards further by the Filberthaugh Bridge. Proceeding up a beautiful ravine we reach the famous 'Trysting Tree', an old decayed gnarled oak with two trunks which unite at the height of 2.13m (7 feet) forming an arch through which lovers could join hands and plight their troth. It received its name as early as 1624. Lying midway between Alnwick Abbey and Hulne Priory it was probably a meeting place for the monks. Half a mile brings us to the Lady's Well and another half mile to the ruins of Hulne Priory.

Hulne Priory was one of the earliest of the Carmelite foundations being founded about 1240 by William de Vesci. Ralph Fresburn, a Northumbrian, was the first prior. Confused legends are told about his adventures in the Crusades and how he chose the site at Alnwick because of its resemblance to Mount Carmel.

By reason of the colour of their vestments the Carmelites were also known as the White Friars. The rules of the Order were very harsh and rigorous. They rose at 5 a.m. in summer and 6 a.m. in winter. Each friar had a coffin in his cell, he slept on straw, and every morning he dug a shovelful of earth for his grave. He crept on his knees to his devotions and spent much time in his cell in silent prayer, he ate twice a day but never tasted animal food. Frequent fasts took place. Their ritual however was carried out on a grand scale and they possessed magnificent robes and vestments. Their library was also unusually large for the time. At Hulne they had one hundred and fourteen manuscripts.

On approaching the ruins the visitor will notice that the curtain wall is complete although it has lost its battlements. It was parapetted with a sentry-walk which was reached by steps from the enclosure, some of which have survived. At the angles were corner turrets which have gone. There were two

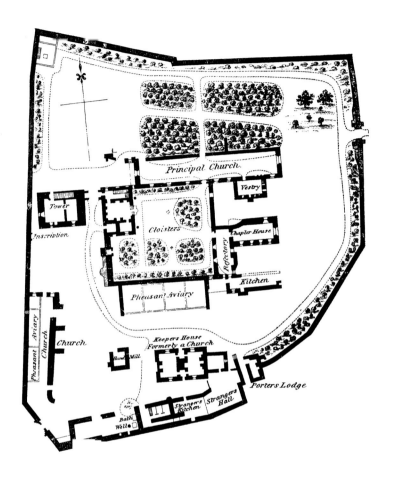

GROUND PLAN
OF
HULNE ABBEY

Surveyed April 1817
by ROB[T] TATE

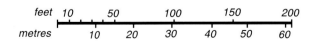

gates, one of which is Tudor. It was guarded by a strong three-storeyed tower. The gateway on the east, which has a lookout and a bell, is dated 1777, the work of the 1st Duke. On each side of the gateway are stone figures of two monks. The modern entrance to the priory is by the south-west door built in 1777.

Entering by the south-west gate and proceeding along the west wall we pass remains of what were once byres and barns and reach the tower. It was built in 1488 by Henry the 4th Earl of Northumberland. Its ground floor is tunnel vaulted. The upper part was gothicized by the 1st Duke, the oriel window being part of his work. In the curtain wall nearby is an inscription, now much decayed, commemorating the building of the tower. A year later the Earl was killed by a mob, protesting at the taxes he was levying. The original tablet is inside the tower, to where it was removed for preservation and a copy placed outside. The total cost of building the tower was £27 19s. 8d.

An archway from the tower leads to what we call the Modern House. It was erected in 1777.

Nearby is the Principal Church which is of great length compared with the width. Practically the whole of the south wall is standing to its full height. Noteworthy are the stepped sedilia (seats) containing the remains of stone figures. In the floor is the unique gravestone bearing the Tau Cross. Generally in crosses representing the wounds of Christ, five nails are shown but here there are only three. The Tau Cross is pre-Christian and is so called because it resembles the Greek T (Tau).

Hulne Abbey from the north-east   W. Davison, 1822

Surrounding the cloisters are grouped the various monastic buildings, including the vestry, chapter house, dormitory and dining hall.

The large detached building which stands just inside the south-west gate was known as the farmery. Above was the granary. By the 19th century it was converted into a dwelling house.

The ruins of Hulne Priory are very picturesque not only for their situation but from the numerous trees and shrubs which are found among the buildings.

BRISLEE TOWER

Crossing the river, below the ruins, by an ornamental iron bridge we proceed up hill in a southerly direction to Brislee or Brislaw Hill which is crowned by Brislee Tower. This ornamental tower in the pseudo-gothic style was erected in 1781 by the first Duke of Northumberland. On it is the following modest inscription in Latin: *Look around! I have measured out all these things, they are my orders, it is my planting; many of these trees have even been planted by my hand.*

THE NINE YEAR AAD HOLE

A quarter of a mile south of Brislee Tower, passing Tower Cottage, is a cave with a strange name. Howitt in his *Visit to Remarkable Places* suggests that this cave is called the Cave of the Nine-Year-Old probably because some celebrated old horse had chosen it, at some period, as his resort; and close by lies Mosstrooper's Field, a hint of former things. The cave is a natural formation. Guarding the entrance is the stone figure of a hermit placed there about 1765. A cave with such a strange name was bound to have its legend.

The legend begins with three robbers who brought there an oaken box filled with stolen gold. They needed food and cast lots as to who should go into Alnwick to buy some. One then went away. Meanwhile the other two dug a hole and buried the treasure. They then discussed how they could get rid of their companion so they could have a larger share of the booty. They made a plan and one of them waylaid their friend who was returning with the bread, and killed him. The murderer returned with the bread but as he stooped to enter the cave was stabbed in the back by the other robber and so there was only one.

However, the robber who had gone to the town in the first place had been thinking of how he could get rid of his two companions. So he had eaten one of the loaves himself and poisoned the two others. When the surviving robber ate some of the bread he died also. There was then no one left to tell where the treasure was hidden.

ALNWICK MARKET

The market and fair at Alnwick was established some time before 1291. The number of fairs varied during the centuries but the most important was called the Alnwick Fair. It was held on the last Monday in July. Writing in 1866 George Tate described the feudal ceremonies associated with this fair in his day.

"The ceremonial commences on the Sunday evening preceding the fair, when the bailiff of the manor, the constables, and other petty officials, representatives of the various townships, and many of the tradesmen of the town, assemble within the castle walls; and having been regaled with wine and ale, march in procession to the Market Cross, where the bailiff proclaims the fair to be held for eight days, and calls over the townships owing suit and service to the barony. Men armed with ancient weapons are placed at the principal entrances of the town, and watch and guard it during the night - a useless precaution since the union of Scotland and England.

"Not content with drinking when they first assembled, the party, after leaving the cross, returned to the castle, and so lavishly was wine distributed among tradesmen in the steward's room, and strong ale to the populace in the court yard, that the quiet and solemnity of the Sunday evening were disturbed by numbers of drunken men bawling, fighting and quarrelling in the streets. Children, too, had their own play during the scene; numbers of them assembled both in front of the castle gates and in the Market Place, abundantly supplied with the cones of pine trees, locally called scrab apples, and with these they pelted each other during the evening, probably a representation of a border fight between the English and Scots. So demoralising and unseemly did this useless Sunday carnival appear to the ministers of religion and others in Alnwick, that they memorialized the duke of Northumberland to put an end to it; and so far was this acceded to, that the refreshments at the castle were discontinued; but the fair is still called and armed men still watch at the gates of the town on the Sunday evening.

"On Monday, the day of the fair, the retainers of the baron assemble about noon in the bailey of the castle, each man mounted; some on gallant well-bred hunters, others on old worn-out mares, some on great rough cart horses, and others on shaggy galloways. After being regaled with strong ale, they leave the castle, headed by the bailiff, who is attended by several men carrying useless old armour, and followed by the duke's piper, dressed in livery, playing some border tune; and after him are marshalled the tenantry. They proceed through the streets of the town; and the bailiff proclaims the fair at the Market Cross, at

St Michael's Pant, where the ancient Grass Cross stood, and at the site of Clayport Tower; and then, in marching order, they return to the castle, where the ceremony is ended by deep draughts of strong Northumbrian ale out of silver flagons."

Alnwick Market Place based on an engraving published by W. Davison, Alnwick 1826

The main market at Alnwick took place on Saturday. In early days no man could buy or sell before the bell tolled eleven o'clock. This bell ringing custom was maintained well into the 19th century but people could start trading at any time they wished. Although the tolls of the markets and fairs were controlled by the lord of the manor the Market Place belonged to the Corporation and they kept it cleaned and in good repair. In 1761 they had the Market Place paved at a cost of almost £11.

Although in Alnwick there were eight or more crosses in the olden time the most important was the Market Cross. From here royal proclamations were made. Here, too, stood the stocks and pillory. The stocks were last used at the beginning of the 19th century.

"Some countrymen, at one of the fairs, had enjoyed themselves too freely, and became uproarous and disorderly; two of them were brought before Charles Grey, and were ordered, as a punishment, to be placed in the stocks for two hours. The boys assembled in great numbers, and pelted the poor countrymen with rotten turnips, cabbage stocks, and other unpleasant missiles; one poor fellow sobbed and wept; but the other clenched his fists and threatened the cruel urchins with a big yarking as soon as he was free".

The original Market Cross was a roofed building supported on pillars. It is mentioned as being repaired in 1629. But it was taken down in 1701. A new building was erected at a cost of £90. We read this cross was "entirely an open building, the roof being supported by pillars; and it was always used for the accommodation of the country people, who came to the market with poultry, butter and eggs".

This cross was demolished in 1763 and replaced by a new shambles or Market House. It was a low building of one storey with an arcade along the north side. It is shown on the engraving published by W. Davison of Alnwick, probably drawn just before its demolition in 1826. The new building was called the Assembly Rooms. Within the arcades on the north and south sides were butchers' shops and above is a large assembly room.

The Market Place - called Markett stede in 1569 - is in the centre of the town. At the west end is the Town Hall and Clock, on the south is the Assembly Hall, on the east is the Town Cross. In Davison's engraving the town cross is shown as a neat structure with seven steps up to the plinth. The shaft is 3m (10')high with a Tuscan capital which is surmounted with four erect dials facing the four cardinal points. But forty years later Tate describes it as "a poor structure having a shaft surmounted by a ball resting on a flight of eight stone steps". The top of the cross today is not in keeping with this ancient and historic pillar.

The Alnwick Fair has been revived. It starts on the last Sunday in May and lasts for a week.

TENANTRY COLUMN

The first object which greets the gaze of the visitor entering Alnwick from the south is a fluted column 25m (83 feet) in height with an internal staircase leading to a gallery at the top. It was designed by David Stephenson in 1816 and was officially called the Tenantry Column.

Many stories have been told about this Column. The best known was told by Charles Harper in his book on the Great North Road. It was quoted in the first edition of this booklet. His story gave rise to the name 'The Farmer's Folly' being applied to this monument. It was erected in honour of the 2nd Duke who was a professional soldier and served in the American War of Independence. Mainly as a result of the Napoleonic Wars there was much distress among the farmers in the county and in January, 1816 the Duke reduced all his tenants' rents by 25%.

Tenantry Column

In the same year it was proposed to erect a column in his honour. Only tenants were allowed to contribute to its cost and 750 of them raised £2,770. Apparently there is no truth to the story that the Duke then raised their rents when he saw what they could afford. The foundation stone was laid on the 1st July, 1816, and here is a description of the ceremony:

"On Ist July, 1816 a procession from the White Swan headed by the Town Band marched to the Column Field. The band was followed by Mr John Pratt, a tenant, carrying a flag with blue and yellow Percy colours with inscriptions; the architect, Mr Stephenson, carrying a scroll of the design and a

29

silver trowel. The principal tenant carried corn, wine and oil, and then the twenty-one oldest tenants paraded carrying white wands with blue and yellow favours on their left breasts. The adjutant of the late Percy Tenantry Volunteers carried a roll of the regiment in a glass case. He was followed by the clergy, then the Chairman of the Subscribers' Committee with Mr Wm. Burrell and His Grace's relations. The committee, with the rest of the tenants, made up the remainder of the procession. The total cost of the ceremony came to £66.4s.5d. including £18.6s.10d. for ale to the local populace at the White Swan.

Medals were struck to commemorate the event. One of gold went to the Duke, and three of silver to Mr Stephenson the architect, Mr Farrington the artist and Mrs Pringle the tenant of the field. The twenty-one oldest tenants received bronze medals and there were also several struck in copper. The building of the column was completed on 12th December, 1818." (Information about the column has been provided by Mr D. P. Graham of Alnwick.)

SCATTERED AROUND the streets of Alnwick are some interesting old buildings which give character to the town.

THE TOWN HALL came into the possession of the corporation in 1585. It was used as a brewhouse, a tolbooth and a guard house. It was rebuilt in 1736 at a cost of £730. The clock spire was raised in 1767 and the 'grand beau window' on the south in 1771. It fronts on Fenkle Street and the Market Place the two places being connected by an arch through the building.

THE SHAMBLES on the side of Northumberland Hall in the market place, were stalls where in medieval times butchers displayed their meat. The term 'shambles' came to mean a flesh market.

THE DUCHESS SCHOOL was built on the site of Derwentwater House, once the possession of the Earl of Derwentwater, executed in 1715. It stands at the corner of Bailiffgate which faces the castle. It is a tall house of five bays built in the late 18th century.

THE CHANTRY Near St Michael's church in Walkergate is a ruined wall, with a moulded doorway and mullioned window. It was founded in 1449 and was more an educational than an ecclesiastical establishment. The two chaplains who resided there not only served at the altar of St Mary in the parish church, but instructed "poor boys in the art of Grammar gratis", and so it was the birthplace of the old Alnwick Grammar School.

ST MICHAEL'S CHURCH The Parish Church of Alnwick is dedicated to St Michael (and originally to St Mary as well). It is first mentioned in 1147 as the Chapel of Alnwick. However, the present church dates from the 15th century. In a charter of Henry VI (1464), the church is mentioned as in need of repair and the rebuilding which followed, in the Perpendicular style of architecture, is basically the church we see today. The chancel, the south wall, the north arcade of the nave and the tower are fine examples of the Perpendicular style. Restorations took place in 1782, 1818 and 1863. In the south-east angle of the chancel is a curious turret containing a circular stone staircase. Originally the home of a chantry priest it would clearly be used in medieval time as a lookout station in connection with Hefferlaw Pele, two-and - a-half miles to the north, where a beacon used to be lit to warn of Scottish raiders.

Alnwick's Church from the south-east   W. Davison, 1822

In the vestry is an ancient muniment chest carved with dragons, a hunting scene, and decorative foliage. It is a 14th century Flemish chest, one of the earliest known to exist in this country. Two bells in the tower are ancient. The oldest (13th century) is inscribed in Latin, translated as follows: *Michael, the archangel, come to the help of the people of God*. The second (15th century) has the inscription, also in Latin, *Hail Mary, full of Grace! Pray ye for the soul of Jolin Valka*. The last name is mutilated and is probably 'Walker'.

Chancel of St Michael's Church

OLD INNS Alnwick, being an important market town on the Great North Road, used to have many old coaching inns and public houses. In 1822 there were "four commodious inns and about thirty public houses". Although extensively altered some have survived to our day.

As we enter Alnwick and approach Bondgate we meet on the right 'Ye Plough Hotel' formerly the Plough Inn. Now rebuilt, it was once a picturesque building with a bay window and the following quaint inscription over the lintel of the doorway: *That which your father old hath purchased and Left you to possess do you dearly Hold to shew his Worthiness. M.W.1714*. The old tablet is still exhibited above the bay window of the new building. The initials are those of Matthew Willoby, the first owner of the house, but the inscription belonged to the Forster family who as early as 1585 used it on their arms.

Passing through the tower, Bondgate Within widens into the Market Place. On the north side is the old White Swan Inn, which is first mentioned in 1729, the hostess being Mrs. Grey. It was the principal coaching inn and here stopped the mail and union coaches. Next door stood a pele tower which was demolished when the Inn was enlarged in the 1850s. The Turk's Head Hotel once stood in Bondgate Within, "distinguished by a projecting wing with a rounded corner".

In Narrowgate is the rival to the White Swan, the Black Swan Inn (in 2001 it became The Hairy Lemon). Here the Northumberland coach used to stop. Further on is the Cross Inn so named from the old De Vescy Cross built into the outer wall. The Half Moon Inn, which is mentioned in 1671, once stood in this street but has now disappeared. Likewise the Three Horse Shoes. The Red Lion Inn (mentioned in 1760) has also vanished from Bailiffgate.

Turk's Head Hotel, c 1900

In Fenkle Street, until almost the end of the 20th century, stood the Nag's Head. It is referred to as early as 1598 under the name of the Griffin, a name it continued to bear in the 18th century. Writing in 1858 George Tate says, "Portions may be from two to three centuries old, its projecting bay window, its stone seat and mount by the side of the outer door, appear much as they were some century and a half ago". The building, with square bay windows, is still there but it is now a shop.

Fenkle Street, based on a sketch published in 1826 by W. Davison

The last house in Bondgate, adjoining to Narrowgate is probably the remains of Alnwick's oldest inn, and if so, the only surviving monastic inn of Northumberland. It is a low building of two storeys with thick walls. In the front wall is a stone panel on which is carved two Percy badges, a crescent with the motto *Esperaunce* and a lion rampant. The lion holds in its paws a shield with two croziers. The croziers connect the building with the abbot of Alnwick Abbey. The combined devices of the Percys and the abbot suggest an ancient monastic hostelry.

THE 'DIRTY BOTTLES' The 18th century Old Cross Inn in Narrowgate is a great attraction to visitors because of the collection of dirty, dusty bottles covered with cobwebs to be seen in the small bow window. We are told that 150 years ago the innkeeper died while dressing the window.

His widow would not have the window cleaned and the legend grew up that if anyone tried to do so he would share the same fate as the landlord. Only one person tried and he died.

The Olde Cross Inn

IN AND AROUND Alnwick are a number of fine old bridges. The finest carries the Great North Road across the River Aln.

LION BRIDGE There was a bridge across the Aln in Norman times, but in 1347 it was in a ruined state and Edward III granted the tolls of this bridge to the men of Alnwick for three years to help them to repair it. "This old bridge, which was standing in the middle of the 18th century, had unusually low battlements and was very narrow, but with a cornered recess on each side over every pier, so that foot passengers might step aside to avoid contact with a vehicle when passing over."

A great flood on the Aln in 1770 seriously damaged the bridge. On the 10th of December the Corporation paid "to John Shepherd 3s. for watching the bridge all last Thursday night to give passengers notice of the danger of going over". A new bridge had to be built about 18m (20 yards) higher up the river in 1773. The architect was John Adam. This bridge has three circular arches, with embattled parapet, and polygonal lookouts. In the middle of the east parapet rises a pedestal on which stands a cast lead lion with a stiff extended tail, similar to that on Northumberland House in London.

DENWICK BRIDGE In the 18th century the road to Denwick was short and direct, crossing the river by a ford. When the 1st Duke of Northumberland extended his park, this road was closed. As compensation the Duke had to make a new road and a bridge across the river. It was built by John Adam, probably at the same time as the Lion Bridge. It is a single arch with the west parapet in the form of Percy crescents and with polygonal lockouts. Because of its graceful arch and surrounding scenery the bridge presents a fine picture.

CANONGATE BRIDGE This bridge, on the Eglingham road, was built in 1821 and has three round arches and a plain parapet. Originally a narrow wooden bridge for foot passengers stood here. It was protected at the sides by wooden railings and rested on stone piers. Horses and carriages passed over by a ford which was dangerous in wet weather. The bridge was destroyed in a flood and had to be replaced in 1821. Mackenzie in 1824 refers to it as "a neat stone bridge of three arches, lately erected near the Abbey Mill".

ON THE OUTSKIRTS of Alnwick there are some interesting buildings associated with the Scottish wars.

ST LEONARD'S HOSPITAL Almost half a mile up the road to Berwick from the Lion Bridge on the left-hand side of the road are the remains of St Leonard's Hospital. It was founded between the years 1193 and 1216 by Eustace de Vescy for the soul of Malcolm King of the Scots, and St Margaret his wife. It was at first an independent religious establishment but in 1376 was annexed by Alnwick Abbey. It probably fell into decay even before the Restoration. It occupies a site in a field called 'Radcliffe's Close', which formerly belonged to the lords of Dilston. The chapel was small consisting of a nave, 6.7m by 8.2m (22 feet by 27 feet), and chancel, 4.6m by 4.9m (15 feet by 16 feet), in the later style of Norman architecture.

Near the north side of the chapel is Malcolm's Well, 1.5m (5 feet) deep, supposed to be the well by the side of which Malcolm drew his last breath.

MALCOLM'S CROSS A little over half a mile up the road to Berwick from the Lion Bridge is Malcolm's Cross standing in a plantation on the right [just before

the roundabout]. Tradition says this is the spot where Malcolm III, the King of Scotland, was slain while besieging Alnwick Castle in 1093. A cross certainly stood here from an early period. But in 1774 it was replaced by the Duchess of Northumberland with the present monument which has been described as of "poor design and workmanship".

Malcolm's Cross with the remains of the old cross in the background.

HEFFERLAW TOWER It is also called Highfarlaw and Heffordlaw and stands on high ground three miles north of Alnwick beside the Great North Road. The pele commands an extensive view and was probably purely military, being used as a watch tower and beacon for Alnwick. It is first mentioned in 1540 as belonging to Alnwick Abbey. It is a small building 7.3m by 8.5m (24 feet by 28 feet) and had three storeys. Set within panels in the walls are two sculptured stones which help us to date the tower. They are similar and one is reproduced here. The crossed croziers are for the abbot, but the crescent and locket are Percy badges. Since they were not used conjointly till the time of the 4th Earl this fixes the date of the tower between 1470 and 1489. The same conjoint badge can be seen on Hedgeley Cross and the porch of Warkworth Church.

Arms sculptured on Hefferlaw Tower

Hefferlaw Tower

WILLIAM DAVISON

No account of Alnwick would be complete without mentioning the great Alnwick printer William Davison (1781-1858). He was an outstanding north country printer who during the 19th century published from his press numerous books and pamphlets of great merit. He has been described as "the most brilliant ornamental printer of his time".

He commenced business as a pharmacist, which he combined with the sale of stationery and printing. His printing career started in partnership with John Catnach, a printer of quality who employed Thomas Bewick to engrave many of his blocks.

Davison became famous for his chapbooks which are now considered to be some of the finest ever published. In 1854 Davison started the first Alnwick newspaper – *Alnwick Mercury* – which when he died had a circulation of 2,600, a remarkable sale for a small provincial newspaper. In 1884 the *Mercury* was amalgamated with the *Alnwick County Gazette* and still continues publication as the weekly *Northumberland Gazette*.

SHROVE TUESDAY FOOTBALL MATCH

Alnwick's Shrove Tuesday football match dates back more than 170 years. Traditionally played between the lads of the parishes of St Paul's and St Michael's the object is to score two goals or 'hales'. Played without obvious strips, or rules, the spectator can be forgiven for not being able to detect two discernible teams. The narrow goal posts, or hales as they are known, are bedecked in green foliage.

The afternoon's events are started by the Duke of Northumberland who drops the match ball from the castle's battlements to the waiting chairman of the Alnwick Shrovetide Football Committee. Then the Duke's piper leads a procession of committee members, players and onlookers over the Lion Bridge and onto the North Demesne where the match is played.

Traditionally the proceedings end with the committee throwing the ball into the river whereupon the more hardy of the players plunge into the Aln's February waters and either by strength, guile or speed one arrives at the far bank as the ball's new owner.

THE DUKE'S PIPER

For almost 250 years there has been a piper to either the Duke or the Duchess of Northumberland. Joseph Turnbull, whose portrait (dated 1756) hangs in Alnwick Castle was the first piper appointed. Later in the 18th century the infamous Jamie Allan held the position. This character was born in a gypsy encampment near Rothbury and learnt both poaching and piping from his father. Charmed by the music of the band he joined the Northumberland Militia but finding the discipline not to his liking soon deserted. Thereafter he spent much time either evading capture or contriving escape, a way of life aggravated by a propensity for enlisting in several regiments from which he deserted in turn. Having broken out of most of the gaols in the north of England he was imprisoned in Durham, for horse stealing, and died there in 1810 just days before the arrival of a free pardon.

A succession of Duke's pipers has continued to present times. Today the only official public duty for the piper is to play at Alnwick's Shrove Tuesday football game although he is required to play for other private occasions.

The Northumbrian small-pipes are the traditional instrument of Northumberland, much quieter and sweeter-sounding than the more familiar bagpipes. In recent years the small-pipes have undergone a revival having once lost out in popularity to the fiddle and accordion. A bagpipe museum is located in Morpeth (a few miles south of Alnwick).

The back cover of this booklet shows a set of Northumbrian small-pipes with seven keys on the chanter and four drones. They are bellows-blown unlike most bagpipes which are mouth-blown. Another notable difference is that the chanter end is closed, this produces their distinctive staccato sound.

Alnwick — A short history and guide by Frank Graham
ISBN 0946928444 This edition 2002
Originally published by Frank Graham
Published by Butler Publishing in 1988 as *Alnwick and Warkworth — A short history and guide*
(ISBN 094692824X). Published as *Alnwick — A short history and guide* in 1994.

The sections 'Shrove Tuesday Football Match' and 'The Duke's Piper' are by Sheena Butler.
Illustrations: Frank Graham, front cover, p 27, p 34(top); Richard Butler, back cover.

© 1988 Butler Publishing, Thropton, Morpeth, Northumberland NE65 7LP

All rights reserved. No part of this publication may be reproduced without the permission of Butler Publishing and the copyright holders.